FROM SEA to SHINING SEA

HAWAI'I

P. J. NERI

Consultants

MELISSA N. MATUSEVICH, PH.D.

Curriculum and Instruction Specialist
Blacksburg, Virginia

DAVE DEL ROCCO AND MAILE DAVIS

Hawai'i State Library
Honolulu, Hawai'i

CHILDREN'S PRESS®

A DIVISION OF SCHOLASTIC INC.

New York • Toronto • London • Auckland • Sydney • Mexico City
New Delhi • Hong Kong • Danbury, Connecticut

Hawai'i is a group of islands in the North Pacific Ocean. The eight major islands are Kaua'i, O'ahu, Maui, Moloka'i, Lāna'i, Kaho'olawe, Ni'ihau, and Hawai'i.

The photograph on the front cover shows a lush rain forest in Manoa Valley on O'ahu.

Project Editor: Meredith DeSousa
Art Director: Marie O'Neill
Photo Researcher: Marybeth Kavanagh
Design: Robin West, Ox and Company, Inc.
Page 6 map and recipe art: Susan Hunt Yule
All other maps: XNR Productions, Inc.

Library of Congress Cataloging-in-Publication Data

Neri, P. J. (Penelope)
  Hawaii / P.J. Neri.
    p. cm. — (From sea to shining sea)
Includes bibliographical references and index.
  ISBN 0-516-22383-6
  1. Hawaii—Juvenile literature. I. Title. II. Series.
  DU623.25 .N47 2003
  996.9—dc21   2002001612

TABLE of CONTENTS

CHAPTER ONE

INTRODUCING THE ALOHA STATE

Hula dancers perform on Waikiki Beach as part of the Aloha Festival, a celebration of all things Hawaiian.

Hawai'i, the fiftieth state, consists of eight islands and 129 islets, reefs, and shoals scattered across 1,500 miles (2,414 kilometers) of the North Pacific Ocean. California is the closest state to Hawai'i, 2,390 miles (3,846 km) to the northeast. The closest country is Japan, 3,850 miles (6,196 km) to the west. These distances make Hawai'i one of the most isolated places on Earth. Even so, Hawai'i residents are some of the friendliest anywhere!

Newcomers to Hawai'i are welcomed with traditional "aloha spirit." *Aloha* is a Hawaiian word that means "love," "hello," or "goodbye." Visitors are given beautiful flower garlands, called *leis,* and a kiss of welcome. It is the friendly aloha spirit of the native people that earned the fiftieth state its nickname, the Aloha State.

The Hawaiian islands were created 3 to 4 million years ago by volcanic eruptions. The islands are an archipelago, or group of islands, in the middle of the Pacific Ocean. There are eight major islands that make up the state. Only seven of these islands are inhabited. They are Ni'ihau, Kaua'i, O'ahu, Moloka'i, Lāna'i, Maui, and Hawai'i. Kaho'olawe is uninhabited.

There are dozens of exciting things to do in Hawai'i. Try snorkeling among colorful coral reefs, or surfing world-famous Waikiki Beach. Learn how to dance the graceful Hawaiian *hula,* or watch a humpback whale flirt its giant tail. In the fiftieth state, you can do all these things and more!

Hawai'i has a mild tropical climate, and some of the most breathtaking scenery in the world. It is not just a great place for tourists, however. The state also has an exciting history that is very different from other states. What comes to mind when you think of Hawai'i?

❖ Polynesian voyagers navigating their canoes by the stars
❖ The bombing of Pearl Harbor
❖ Lava flows and fountains of fire
❖ Hawaiian cowboys
❖ 'Iolani Palace, the only royal palace in the United States
❖ Pineapples, *poi,* and *luaus*
❖ Hula dancing, "grass" skirts, and *ukuleles*
❖ Whales, Hawaiian monk seals, green sea turtles, and sharks
❖ Surfing

Hawai'i has all these things and more. *Aloha! E komo mai!* Welcome to the magical islands of Hawai'i!

Ni'ihau   Kaua'i

O'ahu   ★Honolulu

Moloka'i

Lāna'i

Kaho'olawe

Maui

Hawai'i

6

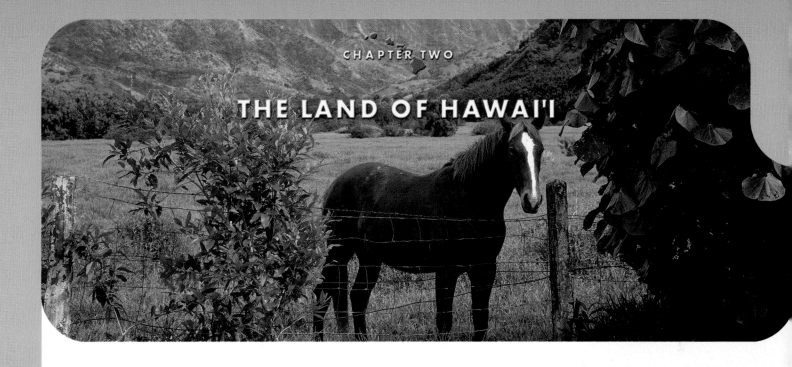

CHAPTER TWO

THE LAND OF HAWAI'I

Hawai'i is an archipelago, or group of islands, that form a curved line across the northern Pacific Ocean. These islands are 2,390 miles (3,846 km) southwest of California. Hawai'i has a total land area of 6,423 square miles (16,636 square kilometers). It ranks forty-seventh in size, compared to the other states.

Although they are called islands, the Hawaiian islands are not islands at all. They are the tops of volcanic mountains. The bottoms of these mountains, called sea mounts, are hidden beneath the ocean. Hawai'i's volcanic mountains are part of a chain of volcanoes called the Pacific Ring of Fire. They were created millions of years ago by violent volcanic eruptions, or explosions.

Eruptions occur when huge plates of earth, called tectonic plates, move toward each other. This movement increases the pressure of gases deep within the Earth's core. As the pressure rises, the gases explode, or

Hawai'i's scenic beauty can be found on all of its islands, including Kaua'i's Lumahai River Valley, shown above.

7

erupt, through cracks in the floor of the ocean. These explosions reach temperatures of over 2000° Fahrenheit (1093° Celsius), hot enough to melt solid rock. This melted rock is called magma, or lava.

The Hawaiian islands were created when boiling lava surged upward through almost 2,000 miles (3,219 km) of cracks in the floor of the Pacific Ocean. As boiling lava met cool ocean water, it hardened. A second layer of lava flowed up and over the first. When this layer cooled and hardened, new land was created on top of the old.

Over millions of years, this happened many times. At last, the tops of the sea mounts appeared above the water as volcanic islands. Even now, another island is "growing" to the southeast of the Big Island of

Lava flows into the Pacific Ocean at Kalapana. The lava enters the ocean at 2100° F (1149° C), and the seawater explodes into steam and boiling water.

Hawai'i. The new island's name is Loihi. Its peaks will not be visible for another ten thousand years.

In the beginning, there was nothing but black rubble on the surface of the islands. Rubble is a mixture of rocks, ash, and cinders that are thrown off by exploding volcanoes. Over thousands of years, heavy rains created rivers that wore away some of the islands' steep mountain ranges. This changed and softened the islands' shape. The rivers also carved out deep valleys, and smoothed volcanic rock into broad flat plains. Meanwhile, the mighty Pacific Ocean ground rocks and seashells into the soft sand of Hawai'i's beaches. When winds, rain, rivers, and oceans wear away and reshape the land, the process is called erosion.

Over thousands of years, storms in distant countries washed logs containing seeds and insects into the ocean. Currents, tides, and winds carried these across many miles of open ocean. Weeks later, the logs washed up on the beaches of the Hawaiian islands. There, the seeds took root in the fertile volcanic ash and sand, and began to grow. Other seeds and insects reached the islands in the droppings or feathers of migrating birds.

EXTRA! EXTRA!

Each of the Hawaiian islands has a nickname, an island color, and an official island flower or shell. Representatives of the islands proudly wear these island symbols during celebrations such as the Aloha Festival, which runs from September to October each year.

Island	Nickname	Color	Flower
O'ahu	The Gathering Place	Yellow	*ilima*
Moloka'i	The Friendly Island	Green	*kukui*
Lāna'i	The Pineapple Island	Orange	*kaunaoa*
Maui	The Valley Island	Pink	*lokelani*
Kaua'i	The Garden Island	Purple	*mokihana*
Hawai'i	The Big Island	Red	*ohia lehua*
Ni'ihau	The Forbidden Island	White	*pupu*, shell
Kaho'olawe	The Forgotten Island	Gray	*hina-hina*

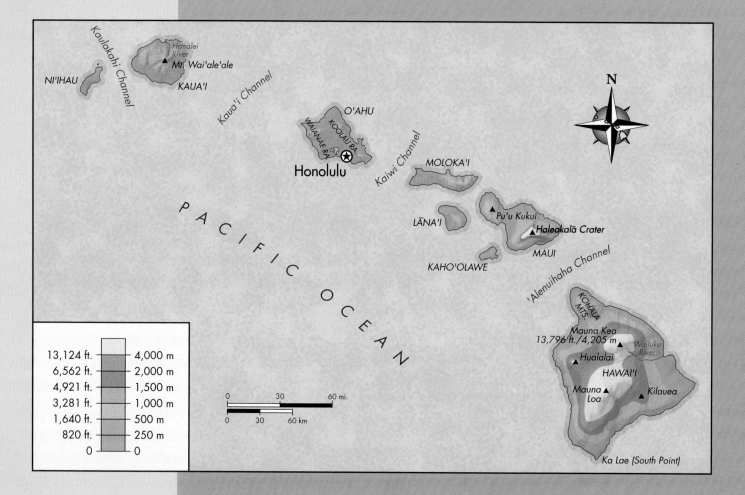

NI'IHAU

Kaulakahi Channel

Hanalei River

Mt. Wai'ale'ale

KAUA'I

Kaua'i Channel

N

O'AHU

WAIANAE RA.
KOOLAU RA.

Honolulu

Kaiwi Channel

MOLOKA'I

Pu'u Kukui

LĀNA'I

Haleakalā Crater

MAUI

KAHO'OLAWE

'Alenuihaha Channel

PACIFIC OCEAN

KOHALA MTS.

Mauna Kea
13,796 ft./4,205 m

Wailuku River

Hualalai

HAWAI'I

Mauna Loa

Kilauea

Ka Lae (South Point)

13,124 ft.	4,000 m
6,562 ft.	2,000 m
4,921 ft.	1,500 m
3,281 ft.	1,000 m
1,640 ft.	500 m
820 ft.	250 m
0	0

0   30   60 mi.

0   30   60 km

Hawai'i's soil is so fertile
that a huge variety of trees,
flowers, and other plants
grow quickly and naturally.

Still others arrived much later, with the first Polynesian settlers, who brought many plants and seeds to the islands. Among these were fruit trees such as banana, breadfruit, and mountain apple trees, or root crops such as sweet potatoes and *taro.* After thousands of years, the bare black rock of the islands was covered in the rich soil, lush vegetation, and exotic flowers we see today.

The island of O'ahu was created 3 to 4 million years ago by the eruption of two volcanoes. Neither of these volcanoes is active now. They are the 4,000-foot (1,219-meter) Waianae Range to the west of O'ahu, and the 3,000-foot (914-m) Ko'olau Range to the east. Over the years, wind and rain have worn away parts of these volcanic mountains to create broad valleys. Erosion has also carved grooves in the slopes of the craggy Ko'olaus. In winter, waterfalls spill down these grooves like silver ribbons.

Rain is not the only form of erosion that shaped the Hawaiian islands. Over the years, the mighty Pacific Ocean surf has ground millions of shells, rock, and chunks of dead coral into the soft powdery sand of Hawai'i's beaches.

CLIMATE

Although Hawai'i is one of the smallest states, it contains several different climate regions. This is because the islands are scattered across 1,500 miles (2,414 km) of ocean. These climate regions range from the tropical rainforests of Hilo, to Kona's dry lava deserts, to Mauna Kea's snowy slopes.

The fiftieth state has only two seasons. They are *Kau,* or summer, and *Ho'oilo,* winter. Island summers last from May to October. The average daytime temperature during summer months is 85° F (29° C). The highest summer temperature on record was a sizzling 100° F (38° C) at Pahala on April 27, 1931. Luckily, the tradewinds blow across the islands from the northeast most of the time. These cooling winds help to make sticky, hot summer days more comfortable for islanders.

Winter lasts from October through April in Hawai'i. The average winter temperature is 78° F (26° C) at sea level. The lowest recorded winter temperature at sea level in the islands was 53° F (12° C). However, at higher elevations, temperatures can be 15 to 30 degrees lower all year round. In

Tourists are attracted by Hawai'i's pleasant, sunny climate. Above, visitors enjoy a day on Waikiki Beach in Honolulu.

A snowboarder flies down the snow-covered slopes of Mauna Kea.

fact, snow covers the high mountain slopes of Mauna Kea, the Big Island's "White Mountain," in winter months. Expert skiers can enjoy skiing down a dormant volcano in the morning and sunbathing on a tropical beach in the afternoon.

Winter is the wettest season, when the islands receive most of their average rainfall of 24 inches (61 centimeters). When warm, damp clouds reach windward mountain slopes, they are carried upward. As they rise, they become cooler and wetter. When the clouds are full of moisture, the moisture falls as rain.

There are two places in the state where the yearly rainfall is much higher than the state average. They are the town of Hilo, on the Big Island, and Mount Wai'ale'ale, on Kaua'i. Hilo receives about 130 inches (330 cm) of rain each year. Not surprisingly, it is the wettest town in the United States.

Kaua'i's Mount Wai'ale'ale is even wetter. In fact, it is the wettest place on Earth! Wai'ale'ale's yearly rainfall averages a soggy 460 inches (1,168 cm). One reason for Mount Wai'ale'ale's record-breaking down-pours is its elevation. Tradewinds at the 600-foot (183-m) level prevent rainclouds from rising. Unable to escape, the clouds are forced to release their moisture as rain.

Winter storms and high winds in the Pacific Ocean send giant waves crashing onto the north shores of the islands. Beautiful Waimea Bay, on O'ahu's North Shore, is world famous for its monster surf, which can measure 25 feet (7.6 m)—twice as high as a school bus. These waves are dangerous for even the best surfers.

June through November is hurricane season in the Pacific Ocean. Although hurricanes rarely hit the Hawaiian islands, there are exceptions. In September 1992, Hurricane Iniki devastated the Aloha State with 175-mile-per-hour (282-kilometer-per-hour) winds. Worst hit was the island of Kaua'i. Six people died as a result of the storm, and more than one hundred were injured. The property damage was also devastating.

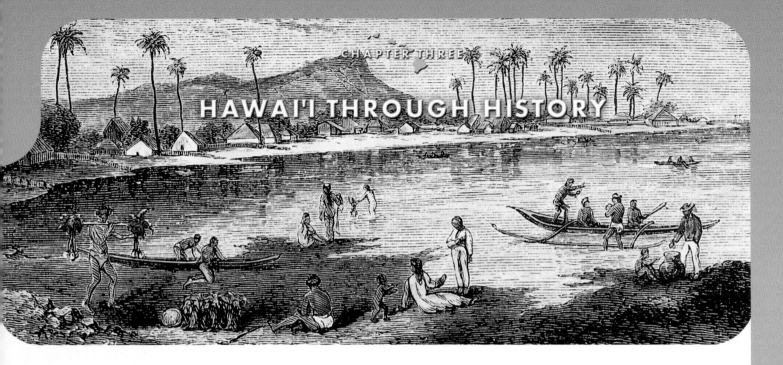

CHAPTER THREE

HAWAI'I THROUGH HISTORY

This drawing shows a settlement at Waikiki in the 1870s.

Between A.D. **500 and** A.D. **700** (although the exact date is unknown), people from an area in the South Pacific known as Polynesia (meaning "many islands") decided to leave their homelands. Loading their beloved families, animals, and plants onto double-hulled voyaging canoes, they set sail in search of a new place to live.

The brave Polynesian pioneers sailed their canoes northwest, crossing 2,000 miles (3,219 km) of unknown ocean. They had no maps to show them the way. Instead, they used the position of the stars in the night sky as a map. The flight of passing seabirds, the direction of the wind, and the changing ocean currents also showed these expert sailors where to find land.

After weeks at sea, the tired voyagers reached a chain of beautiful green islands and decided to make them their home. They called them *Hawaiki*, probably after the homeland they had left behind.

EARLY HAWAIIAN SETTLERS

The first Hawaiian settlers wasted no time planting the seeds and plants they had brought with them. These included taro roots and sweet potatoes, coconut trees, banana trees, breadfruit, mountain apples, and sugarcane. They built huts thatched with grass, called *pili,* for shelter against the sun and rain.

Each family lived, worked, and traded with others in an *ahupua'a,* a division of land. Every ahupua'a reached from the mountain to the sea. If properly planted and cared for, the land would provide enough food for everyone in that community.

Extended families, called *'ohana,* worked together, side by side. They planted patches of land with taro roots, burying the corms deep in the fertile mud. They dug ditches to water their crops, and raised pigs and chickens. Native Hawaiians also built ponds in which they raised fish, enclosing them with low walls built of lava rocks. These foods, along with other fish and sea creatures, provided Native Hawaiians with a varied diet. Like the Native Americans, they lived in harmony with their beloved *aina* (land).

The early Hawaiians were divided into social classes. Each island had several chieftans called

A group of islanders canoe in the North Pacific.

ali'i, who ruled over the people of their provinces. The common people were called *maka'ainana.* Most of them were either farmers or fishermen. Below the ali'i were the *kahuna* class, or priests.

Some kahuna taught canoe building, hula dancing, and other special skills. Other kahuna were in charge of religious matters. They built temples, called *heiau,* to honor the Hawaiian gods. These were places where rituals could be held and offerings could be made. Each family also had a special family guardian, such as the shark, turtle, or owl. The people believed that these guardians, called *aumakua,* protected the family.

At this time, there was no written Hawaiian language and no schools. Young Hawaiians learned the history of their people by word of mouth, usually from the chants of the kahuna or from the *kupuna* (old ones).

A high chieftain called the *ali'i nui* ruled each island. The people believed that these high chieftains were descended from the gods. The ali'i nui had the power of life and death over everyone. They could also give or take away land and wealth as they chose.

The high chieftains and the priests made laws, called *kapus.* Some of these laws were very harsh. For example, one kapu said that men and women should not eat together. Another law said that if the shadow of an ordinary person fell across a high chief, the ordinary person was to be killed immediately.

If someone broke a kapu, his or her only hope of survival was to escape to a place of refuge. If the person reached the place without being captured, he or she was allowed to live. One of these safe places still stands at Honaunau, on the Big Island.

Native Hawaiians enjoyed surfing and swimming along the coast.

Despite strict laws, there was still time for people to celebrate and have fun. During the four months of the *makahiki,* or harvest season, the people gave thanks to Lono, god of the harvest. They also played games such as *konane,* which is similar to checkers. The Hawaiians also held boxing, wrestling, spear-throwing, and canoe-racing contests.

Hawaiian men and women also enjoyed bodysurfing and board surfing, both invented by the Polynesians. Unlike modern surfboards, which are made of lightweight fiberglass, the earliest surfboards were made of wood from the koa tree. They were more than 6 feet (1.8 m) long and very heavy.

ARRIVAL OF THE EUROPEANS

In January 1778, British explorer Captain James Cook anchored his sailing ship off Waimea, Kaua'i. Cook was returning from his exploration of the northwest Pacific when he became the first European explorer on record to visit Hawai'i.

The Hawaiians paddled their canoes out to meet Cook's ship. Its white sails looked very similar to the white banners of their harvest god, Lono. Believing Captain Cook was Lono, the Hawaiians treated Cook and his crew as honored guests. They gave them fruit, pigs, fresh water,

The islanders greeted Captain Cook with great ceremony.

and many other gifts. Cook claimed the islands as British territory. He named them the Sandwich Islands after his employer, the Earl of Sandwich.

Captain Cook visited Hawai'i again the following year. This time, he dropped anchor off the Big Island's Kealakekua Bay. By this time, Hawaiians no longer believed that the British captain was a god. One night, some of them stole one of Cook's boats. The crew fired shots at the thieves, and a fight broke out. During the fight, Captain Cook was clubbed over the head and killed. Cook's crew killed many Hawaiians in revenge for their captain's death. Afterwards, the crew returned to England without their captain.

The Hawaiians were relieved when the Europeans left. The westerners had not respected the kapus of the Hawaiian people. They had also unknowingly brought with them contagious diseases such as cholera and measles. The Polynesians had no immunity against these diseases. After the westerners left Hawai'i, thousands of Hawaiians died of these and other diseases.

NEW ARRIVALS

Once westerners discovered the islands, ships came to Hawai'i from all over the world. Some of these ships belonged to traders on their way to China, where they traded western goods for silks and spices.

Most western traders were interested in the huge forests of sandalwood growing in Hawai'i's mountains. The traders knew that the Chinese burned this sweet-smelling wood during religious ceremonies, and that they would pay very well for it. From about 1805 to 1830, Hawai'i's chiefs traded sandalwood in return for western luxuries and weapons. In just twenty-five years, the islands' sandalwood forests had vanished.

THE REIGN OF KAMEHAMEHA THE GREAT

At this time, each island was ruled by its own chieftain. Despite this, a young Hawaiian chieftain named Kamehameha wanted to unite all of the islands under his rule. He and his army captured each island, and by 1795, only O'ahu, Kaua'i, and Ni'ihau remained unconquered. In a fierce battle, Kamehameha's warriors pushed their enemies to their deaths over the towering cliffs of Nu'uanu Pali, on the island of O'ahu. In 1810, Kamehameha gained control of Kaua'i and Ni'ihau by coming to an agreement with their chieftains. For uniting all of the islands under his rule, Kamehameha earned the title Kamehameha the Great.

In 1793, British sea captain George Vancouver brought a gift for Kamehameha from England. He brought the first cattle to the islands

WHO'S WHO IN HAWAI'I?

Kamehameha the Great (1758–1819) was the first Hawaiian King. His name, *Kamehameha* (Ka-may-ha-may-ha), means "the lonely one." The state remembers Kamehameha's birthday each year on June 11. This state holiday is celebrated with a parade of flower floats, marching bands, and Hawaiian riders.

by ship. However, after so many weeks at sea, many of the cattle were either dead or dying.

King Kamehameha placed a ten-year ban on the sickly cows. No one was allowed to touch the animals during that time. In just a few years, thousands of long-horned cattle were running wild in Hawai'i's mountains. Some trampled crops and injured people in the villages. Kamehameha knew something had to be done to control the cattle.

John Parker, a sailor from Connecticut, offered to help. Parker rounded up and tamed the wild cattle on the Big Island. To help manage the cattle, Parker brought Spanish cowboys to his ranch in the northwest corner of the island. Their job was to teach the Hawaiians how to herd cattle. The cowboys called themselves *españoles*. This word,

Modern-day Hawaiian cowboys, still referred to as paniolo, herd cattle on the Parker Ranch.

which means "Spanish," soon became *paniolo* in Hawaiian.

Once a year, the paniolo at Parker Ranch herded cattle down from the mountains to the seashore. The paniolo swam alongside one cow at a time to waiting cattle boats. The cattle were lifted aboard the boats by a crane, then shipped to cattle markets on O'ahu. The loading was done this way because the water was too shallow for cattle boats to come closer to shore. Herding frightened long-horned cattle in deep water was difficult and dangerous work.

THE END OF THE KAPU SYSTEM

After King Kamehameha died in 1819, Queen Ka'ahumanu ruled the islands in his place. However, the queen did not want to follow old laws that prevented women from doing many things that men were allowed to do. Queen Ka'ahumanu decided to break the kapus by eating a meal with the men in her family.

The native Hawaiian people were shocked when they saw their queen disobeying the kapus. They expected the gods to punish her. However, when nothing happened, the people also broke the old laws and abandoned their gods.

With their religion and laws gone, Hawaiians felt alone and bewildered. It was at this time that members of the Congregational Church of Massachusetts began making plans to send Christian missionaries to Hawai'i. (Missionaries are people who teach their religious beliefs to others.) The missionaries hoped to convert, or change, the Hawaiian people to the Christian religion. The first missionaries arrived on April 19, 1820, aboard the sailing ship *Thaddeus.* Their leader was Reverend Hiram Bingham.

The missionaries immediately began teaching Hawaiians about the Christian religion. They also translated the Christian Bible into the Hawaiian language. This was very difficult because Hawaiian had never

WHO'S WHO IN HAWAI'I?

Father Damien (1840–1889) was a Catholic missionary priest from Belgium. He arrived in Hawai'i in 1873 and took care of leprosy victims on Moloka'i's Kalaupapa Peninsula. Leprosy was an incurable disease, and people who contracted it were often left to die at Kalaupapa. The Kalaupapa Peninsula is now a National Historic Site. A statue of Father Damien stands in the nation's capitol in Washington, D.C.

A missionary preaches in the shade of kukui trees.

been written. The missionaries wrote a Hawaiian alphabet and decided that each English letter would represent a sound used in the Hawaiian language. However, unlike the English alphabet, the Hawaiian alphabet had only twelve letters—five vowels and seven consonants. Symbols called 'okina and kahako, which help in pronunciation, were added later.

The missionaries started the first schools in the islands called *kula.* Classes were held beneath shady shelters of palm leaves or *pili* grass. Before long, most Hawaiians could read and write Hawaiian, and speak English.

To encourage Hawaiians to use English, the missionaries did not allow Hawaiian to be spoken during school hours. The missionaries also banned the traditional Hawaiian hula dance, because they believed that the hula was a reminder of the Hawaiians' non-Christian religion. Although the dance was banned, however, many Hawaiians continued to dance hula in private.

Native Hawaiians present a hula dance in the mid-1850s.

In 1819, the first whaling ships came to Hawai'i. In those days, people burned oil in lamps or lanterns to light their homes. The oil came from the fat, or blubber, of whales. Whaling captains and their crews killed thousands of humpback whales every year in Hawaiian waters.

By 1850, there were more than five hundred ships hunting whales in island waters each year. Honolulu on O'ahu, and Lahaina on Maui quickly became the sailors' favorite ports. However, the sailors were not well-liked by the missionaries. After spending many months at sea, the seamen were noisy and rowdy when they came ashore. This led to heated arguments with the missionaries. Sailors often ended up in jail, which Hawaiians called the "Stuck-in-Irons" house. On one occasion, angry sailors fired their ship's cannon at the missionaries' homes on Front Street in Lahaina.

In just over fifty years, most of the whales in Hawaiian waters had been harpooned for their oil. As suddenly as they arrived, the whalers left Hawai'i to hunt whales in other waters.

Whalers braved the high seas in hopes of earning huge profits.

25

THE GREAT MAHELE

By 1826, the United States officially recognized Hawai'i as an independent kingdom. In 1840, Kamehameha III established Hawai'i's first constitution as the Kingdom of Hawai'i.

Until 1848, all of Hawai'i's land belonged to the king. After that, the king proclaimed a new law called the Great Mahele, or land division. Under the Great Mahele, some of the king's land was offered to the royal family. Some of the land that was left was divided into farms averaging about 3 acres (1.2 hectares) for the Hawaiian people. These farms were called *kuleanas*.

The Great Mahele seemed like a good idea. However, in just a few decades, 8 in every 10 Native Hawaiians had been tricked into selling their kuleanas to non-Hawaiians for very little money. Former missionaries became wealthy landowners almost overnight by marrying the daughters of Hawaiian royalty, or chieftains.

Before long, these landowners realized that growing crops such as sugarcane and pineapple could make their land very profitable. Within a few years, five of these families started companies that owned and controlled most of the sugarcane and pineapple plantations in the islands. These companies were AMFAC, C. Brewer, Alexan-

This illustration shows the village of Waikiki in the mid-1800s.

der and Baldwin, Castle & Cooke, and Theo H. Davies. These family companies became known as "The Big Five." The Big Five controlled Hawai'i's agriculture for decades.

THE SWEETEST CROP

By 1835, huge fields of sugarcane seedlings were planted in the flattest, wettest areas of Hawai'i, such as the central plains of O'ahu and the Hamakua Coast of the Big Island. Hundreds of laborers were needed to plant, care for, and harvest the sugarcane. Over the next fifty years, plantation owners brought more than 300,000 immigrant laborers to the islands from China, Japan, and Portugal. These immigrants quickly outnumbered Native Hawaiians.

Before long, so many different languages were being spoken in Hawai'i that the laborers could not understand each other. A new language that everyone knew and could understand was needed. The result was *pidgin* English, which is still spoken in the islands today. Pidgin is a combination of many different languages.

Plantation towns, called camps, grew up around different immigrant groups, such as the Filipino camp, or the Japanese camp. The sugar plantation companies owned the workers' homes. The sugar companies also owned plantation stores, where workers bought food and everything else they needed. By controlling their work, pay, and daily life, the plantation was able to control its laborers.

Plantation owners also built railroads to transport the sugarcane to mills for processing. After this, the sugar was shipped to the United States. At the time, foreign countries like Hawai'i had to pay a high tax to sell their sugar in the United States. If Hawai'i was part of the United States, the planters would not have to pay this tax. However, the only way they could make this happen was by overthrowing the Hawaiian monarchy.

THE RECIPROCITY TREATY

By 1871, Hawai'i's economic future was uncertain. Hawai'i's income from the whaling industry ended when oil was found in Pennsylvania. Petroleum oil quickly replaced whale oil. Sugar became Hawai'i's most promising industry. However, sugar entering the United States was still heavily taxed.

In 1875, King Kalākaua signed what is known as the Reciprocity Treaty with the United States. (*Reciprocity* means that something is given in return for something else.) Under this treaty, Hawaiian sugar could be imported into the United States free of tax. In return, United States' products were brought into Hawai'i tax-free. This treaty led to a huge increase in Hawai'i's sugar production. It was a good start, but not enough for greedy American planters.

King Kalākaua was popular among Hawaiians for other reasons. He brought back the beloved hula, which the missionaries had banned. He also built 'Iolani Palace, the only royal palace in the United States. Kalākaua also wrote the song "Hawai'i Pono'i," which later became the state anthem.

Despite the Reciprocity Treaty and the king's popularity with his people, American businessmen in Hawai'i disliked Kalākaua. In 1887, they persuaded him to sign a new constitution. This constitution limited his powers as king. It later became known as the Bayonet Constitution.

King Kalākaua was known as the Merry Monarch because of his interest in dance and music.

REBELLION

In 1889, Native Hawaiians, led by part-Hawaiian Robert Wilcox, tried to take over 'Iolani Palace. They hoped to overturn the Bayonet Constitution and return control to their king. However, this rebellion, called the Wilcox Rebellion, failed. Those who had taken part in it were arrested and imprisoned.

In 1891, King Kalākaua died unexpectedly in San Francisco. His sister, Lili'uokalani, became queen. Queen Lili'uokalani believed her brother had given Americans too much control in Hawai'i's government. She wanted her people to decide for themselves how their kingdom would be governed.

Rumors spread that the new queen planned to make foreigners leave Hawai'i. American planters were afraid that they would lose their sugar plantations. To prevent this, a group of American businessmen decided to overthrow the Hawaiian government and make Hawai'i a United States territory. These men were called annexationists.

Judge Sanford B. Dole, leader of the annexationists, led the takeover. With the help of the U.S. Ambassador, the U.S. Marines, and the U.S. Navy, Dole and other annexationists arrested Queen Lili'uokalani. She was imprisoned in 'Iolani Palace. In the one hundred years since the Europeans first visited the little kingdom, the Hawaiians lost their gods, laws, health, land, religion, and culture. Now they had lost their beloved queen.

Sanford B. Dole was inaugurated as governor on June 14, 1900.

When United States President Grover Cleveland heard that Americans had overthrown the queen, he was very angry. The president insisted that Dole return control of Hawai'i to Lili'uokalani and restore the Hawaiian government. However, Congress (the lawmaking body of the United States government) allowed Hawai'i's government to be replaced by a provisional, or temporary, government. Dole headed this new republic.

Despite the protests of more than 21,000 Native Hawaiians, Hawai'i was made a United States territory in 1900. The joint resolution, or law, to approve this was signed by President William McKinley, and passed in Congress. Dole was appointed Hawai'i's first territorial governor.

Soon after Hawai'i became a United States territory, several U.S. military bases were established there, including Pearl Harbor, on the island of O'ahu. Pearl Harbor soon became home to the ships of the U.S. Pacific fleet.

PLAGUE AND FIRE IN CHINATOWN

In December 1899, several people in Honolulu died of a mysterious illness. These people were killed by bubonic plague, a disease that is spread quickly by rats and fleas. More than half the infected people lived in Honolulu's crowded Chinatown area.

The Board of Health decided to try "controlled burnings" in an attempt to kill the plague germs. They hoped that by burning buildings where the disease was found, they could stop the plague from spreading.

Terrified Chinatown residents watched as their belongings, homes, and businesses were burned to the ground by the Honolulu fire department. However, on January 20, 1900, the wind changed direction and the fire spread out of control. Hungry flames leaped from building to building. Afraid they would be burned, people desperately tried to escape from Chinatown.

Armed soldiers and policemen surrounded the area. They would not let anyone leave. Instead, four thousand residents were locked in the grounds of the Kawaiaha'o Church until the terrible fire had burned itself out. Before it was over, the fire had destroyed eight city blocks and left seven thousand people homeless. It would be several years before Chinatown recovered.

HAWAI'I IN THE TWENTIETH CENTURY

In 1917, Native Hawaiians mourned the death of Lili'uokalani, who died peacefully at her home at Washington Place. After her death, Washington Place became the official Honolulu residence of Hawai'i's governors.

EXTRA! EXTRA!

In 2002, construction began on a new governor's residence in Honolulu. Once it is completed, Washington Place will become a museum.

By 1900, growing pineapple had become Hawai'i's second most successful business after sugar. The most successful pineapple grower was the "Pineapple King," James D. Dole, the cousin of Hawai'i's territorial governor, Sanford B. Dole.

Dole started his first pineapple plantation in Wahiawa, O'ahu, in 1901. In 1922, he bought the entire island of Lāna'i on which to grow pineapple. Laborers were brought from Puerto Rico, the Philippines, and Korea to work in the fields. Pineapple remained Lāna'i's only industry until 1992, when the last crop was harvested.

Life was good for plantation owners, but very difficult for the workers. While company owners lived in luxurious mansions, the average plantation worker and his family lived in cramped wooden houses owned by the plantation. Plantation workers received less than 30 cents per hour for their backbreaking labor, and many were deeply in debt to plantation stores.

By 1946, Hawai'i's 28,000 sugar plantation workers joined a labor union called the International Longshore and Warehouse Union (ILWU). The union helped organize laborers to fight for better wages and improved working and living conditions. To get their point across, the workers went on strike and refused to work until their demands were met. The strike was successful.

Dole became known as the "Pineapple King" because he was able to successfully grow pineapple where others had failed.

A family of Native Hawaiians sits outside their pili grass hut in Honolulu in 1900.

TOURISM IN HAWAI'I

Mark Twain, the famous American writer, was the first tourist to fall in love with Hawai'i as early as 1866. "For me, its balmy airs are always blowing," Twain wrote, "its summer seas flashing in the sun; the pulsing of its surfbeat is in my ear: I can see its garlanded crags, its leaping cascades, its plumy palms drowsing by the shore. . . ." Like those who came after him, Twain never forgot the islands' beauty.

Hawai'i's tourism industry officially began in 1927. That year, the first luxury passenger ship, the S.S. *Malolo*, began voyages between San Francisco and the islands. On Boat Days, Hawaiians crowded Honolulu Harbor to greet the ships and the new arrivals with flower leis and welcoming cries of "Aloha!" Brass bands played, and young people dived for coins thrown into Honolulu Harbor from the decks of the ships. By 1941, Pan American planes brought visitors from San Francisco to Hawai'i each day.

THE BOMBING OF PEARL HARBOR

All passenger flights and sea voyages stopped in December 1941, when the unthinkable happened. On December 7, Japanese planes bombed the U.S. Navy's Pacific Fleet in Pearl Harbor. They attacked without warning, killing 2,500 people. Japanese bombers also sank the USS *Arizona*, along with her crew of almost 1,200 men.

The attack on Pearl Harbor forced the United States to fight against Japan in World War II (1939–1945). It also made everyone suspicious

of Japanese Americans. Japanese Americans who held important positions in Hawai'i lost their jobs. If they owned businesses and stores, these were taken away from them. People were told not to trust Japanese Americans.

A launch boat rescues a sailor as the USS *West Virginia* burns after the attack on Pearl Harbor.

To prove that they were loyal to America, thousands of Japanese Americans volunteered to fight in World War II. Half of these soldiers belonged to the famed 442nd Regiment. This combat regiment won more medals for bravery than any other unit in United States history.

STATEHOOD

On August 21, 1959, President Dwight D. Eisenhower proclaimed Hawai'i the fiftieth state of the Union. After statehood, Hawai'i's economy flourished for several years. Hawai'i's income from tourism was particularly high after 1985, thanks to millions of yearly visitors from Japan and Korea. However, Hawai'i's tourism dropped off sharply after 1995, when Asian countries experienced severe economic problems. Asian tourists could no longer afford vacations in Hawai'i. As a result, Hawai'i's airlines, hotels, stores, and service industries suffered heavy losses.

Tourism declined even more after the tragedy of September 11, 2001, when terrorists hijacked commercial airplanes and attacked New York's World Trade Center and the Pentagon in Washington, D.C. The attacks killed thousands of innocent people. Such terrible loss of life and destruction reminded many people of the 1941 attack on Pearl Harbor.

Many months later, people were still afraid to travel by air. Thousands of family vacations, business trips, and trade conventions were canceled. Service industries, such as hotels, banks, and restaurants, also suffered. Many island residents lost their businesses and jobs during this time. Almost 5 in every 100 people in Hawai'i are still unemployed.

Although wages are lower in the fiftieth state than they are on the mainland, the cost of island living is higher. Most Hawai'i residents are willing to pay the higher cost of living because of their love for the islands. However, not everyone can afford to make this choice. Thousands of residents leave the islands each year to find better paying jobs on the mainland. Most affected are Native Hawaiians, who have the lowest income in the state. They also have the highest rates of illness and other social problems.

Hawai'i's economy will most likely improve when tourists are reassured that air travel is safe again. When that happens, tourists will find the aloha spirit waiting to greet them in Hawai'i.

Native Hawaiians make up fewer than one-quarter of Hawai'i's total population.

CHAPTER FOUR

GOVERNING HAWAI'I

The Hawaiian capitol is admired for its symbolic design.

EXTRA! EXTRA!

Hawai'i has four counties: Maui (which runs the islands of Maui, Kaho'olawe, Moloka'i and Lāna'i); Kaua'i (which runs Kaua'i and Ni'ihau); Honolulu; and Hawai'i. A mayor is chosen to run each county, with the advice of his or her county council.

The eight major islands are governed by the state constitution. A constitution contains the state's rules and laws, and determines how the state should be organized. Hawai'i's constitution was written in 1950 and has been amended, or changed, several times.

The constitution divides Hawai'i's state government into three parts, or branches. They are the executive branch, the legislative branch, and the judicial branch. Unlike other states, there is no separate municipal, or city, government in the fiftieth state. Hawai'i's cities and counties are run by mayors.

EXECUTIVE BRANCH

The executive branch makes sure that the state's laws are being carried out. The governor is head of the executive branch. He or she is elected by state residents to serve a four-year term. The governor, the lieutenant governor, the attorney general, and seventeen state departments make up the executive branch of Hawai'i's government. They work together to make sure the state runs smoothly.

LEGISLATIVE BRANCH

The legislative branch makes state laws. Laws may be about a wide range of issues, such as building new public schools and highways, or setting aside money for new parks.

The legislative branch is divided into two parts, called houses: the house of representatives and the senate. Fifty-one representatives serve two-year terms. Twenty-five elected senators serve four-year terms. The legislature meets once per year in January.

Senators and representatives are chosen by the people. Responsible citizens vote for representatives who think as they do about important matters. You can find out how a representative feels about these issues

When the legislature is in session, the house chamber (above) is filled with lawmakers in lively discussion.

HAWAI'I GOVERNORS

Name	Term	Name	Term
William F. Quinn	1959–1962	John Waihee	1986–1994
John A. Burns	1962–1974	Benjamin J. Cayetano	1994–
George R. Ariyoshi	1974–1986		

by listening to his or her campaign speeches and by asking questions. The right to vote gives every person the chance to say how his or her state should be governed.

JUDICIAL BRANCH

Hawai'i's judicial branch interprets, or explains, the law and punishes lawbreakers. Different courts hear different types of cases. These courts include the supreme court, district courts, family courts, circuit courts, tax appeal court, land court, and the intermediate court of appeals. Hawai'i's supreme court is the highest, or most important, court in the state. Five supreme court justices (judges) are chosen by the governor and approved by the senate.

HAWAI'I STATE GOVERNMENT

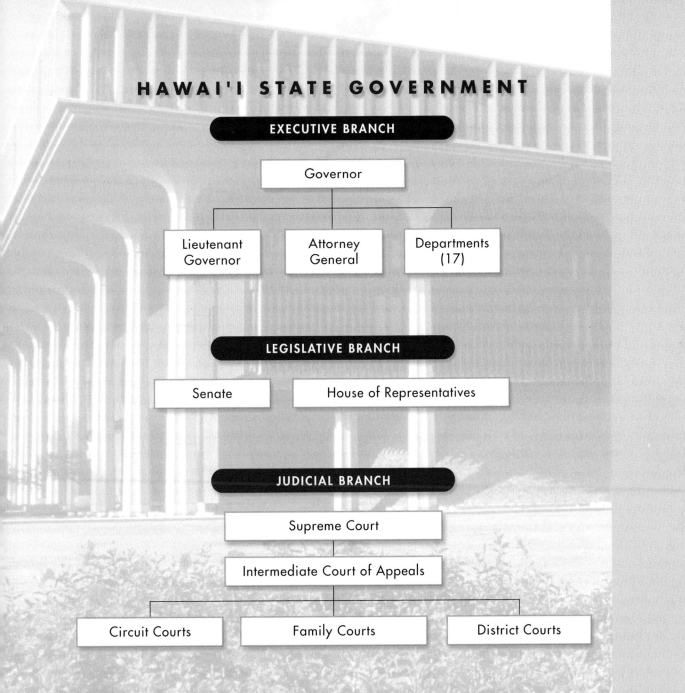

EXECUTIVE BRANCH

Governor

Lieutenant Governor

Attorney General

Departments (17)

LEGISLATIVE BRANCH

Senate

House of Representatives

JUDICIAL BRANCH

Supreme Court

Intermediate Court of Appeals

Circuit Courts

Family Courts

District Courts

Let's begin our tour of Honolulu at the state capitol, a beautiful, airy building that was designed to look like the islands it represents. Its roofs are cone-shaped, a reminder that the islands were created by volcanoes. It has tall, slender pillars that represent the island's palm trees. Ponds surround the capitol, just as the Pacific Ocean surrounds the islands. Open courtyards allow cooling tradewinds to pass through the capitol building.

'Iolani Palace is located on King Street. It looks like a white dollhouse, with graceful steps and verandahs around the top and bottom floors. The palace is surrounded by lawns and elegant stone walls topped with wrought iron. Built during the reign of King Kalākaua, it was originally the home of Hawaiian kings and queens. After the overthrow of the monarchy in 1893, the palace was used as the state capitol. It is now a museum and is being restored.

'Iolani Palace is the only royal palace in the United States.

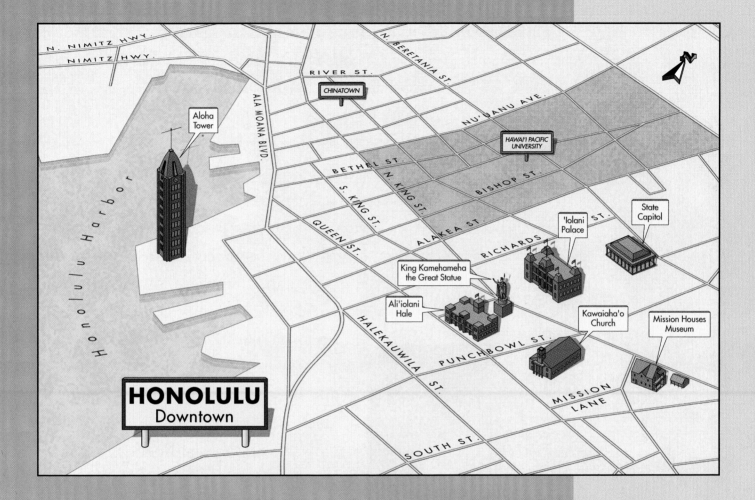

As you leave the palace gates, walk across the street to the huge statue of King Kamehameha the Great, sculpted by Thomas Gould in 1880. Hundreds of flower leis hang from the king's outstretched arms on Kamehameha Day, a state holiday that commemorates the King's birthday. Kamehameha's statue stands in front of Ali'iolani Hale (*ha-lay*), the first government building on the island.

The Mission Houses Museum is nearby. The mission houses are among the oldest wooden buildings on the islands. They were brought to the islands in pieces aboard sailing ships, then put together like jigsaw puzzles. These wooden houses were the homes of O'ahu's first missionaries. They are filled with missionary belongings, furniture from the 1800s, and an old printing press. Other items include children's toys and furniture, Hawaiian quilts, and early prayer books.

The mission houses were built in the early 1800s. Three of the original structures still remain on the site.

Across the street from the Mission Houses Museum is the Kawaiaha'o Church. Built between 1836 and 1842, this is O'ahu's oldest Christian church. Kawaiaha'o was built of coral blocks brought up from the ocean. Hawaiian royalty once worshipped there. At the church's graveyard, hundreds of interesting inscriptions on the gravestones date back to the earliest missionary times.

Just five blocks away, overlooking the Honolulu Harbor, is the Aloha Tower. Built in the early 1900s, the tower is ten stories tall. Originally part of a steamer terminal, it was once the tallest landmark in Honolulu. The Tower has two clocks; one faces the ocean and the other faces the island. Below the clock, the word *Aloha* greets tourists arriving by ocean steamer. At the base of the tower, a beautiful shopping center now overlooks the harbor.

Chinatown is the next stop on our tour. Although almost all of the original Chinatown was destroyed in the Great Fire, it has been rebuilt since then. Everywhere you look there are temples, herb shops, noodle shops, and storefronts decorated with good-luck dragon designs, or Chinese characters representing prosperity and wealth. Chinatown's grocery and meat markets offer exotic choices of vegetables and meats. You'll find sweet *char-siu* red pork, fiery Korean *kim chee,* or pickled cabbage, pickled pig's head or feet, and whole red Peking ducks. Stop at the Maunakea Marketplace for something good to eat. *Manapua* (steamed rice-flour buns filled with tasty shredded pork and vegetables) or a bowl of Vietnamese *pho* noodles will make a great lunch to end our walking tour of downtown Honolulu.

The Aloha Tower is a familiar landmark in Honolulu's skyline.

CHAPTER FIVE

THE PEOPLE AND PLACES OF HAWAI'I

Young Hawaiians participate in a Christmas hula show in Honolulu.

According to the **2000 census,** the population of Hawai'i is 1,211,537. It ranks forty-second compared to other states. Hawai'i's cultural diversity is greater than any other state in the country. More than 1 in every 5 people have a mixed ethnic background. Almost 42 in every 100 people are Asian, 24 in every 100 are of European descent, 7 in every 100 are Hispanic, and just under 2 in 100 are African-American. About 10 in every 100 people are Native Hawaiian or Pacific Islanders. However, there are fewer than 10,000 full-blooded Native Hawaiians living today.

The variety of people in the fiftieth state has created an unusual and exciting cultural blend. An island potluck may include Chinese fried noodles; Filipino *lumpia*, or eggrolls; Portuguese bean soup; Mexican enchiladas; Japanese sushi; Puerto Rican *pasteles*, or meat-filled treats; and Hawaiian *kalua*, or roasted pig. Most people in Hawai'i adopt a mixture of Hawaiian, Chinese, Japanese, or Filipino traditions to suit their tastes.

Traditional native Hawaiian feasts, called luaus, are held in honor of graduations, weddings, or a baby's first birthday. The feast includes shredded pork cooked in an underground oven called an *imu*, *poi* made from taro roots, and *lomi-lomi* salmon with diced tomatoes and onions. These and other delicious foods are followed by a dessert of *haupia*, or coconut pudding, and fresh pineapple.

The luau has become a popular tourist event. Here, a crowd gathers to watch the imu ceremony at the Old Lahaina Luau.

SPORTS IN HAWAI'I

Sports are enjoyed year round in Hawai'i, thanks to the sunny weather. Sports played in the islands include soccer, football, baseball, basketball, and volleyball. Water sports, such as windsurfing, swimming, canoe paddling, and board surfing, are also popular.

Surfing was invented by Hawaiians. Ancient Hawaiians surfed using heavy koa-wood surfboards. Modern surfers use colorful boards made of lightweight fiberglass, or resin. There are several excellent surfing beaches in the islands. Two of the most

EXTRA! EXTRA!

Surfers have their own language with strange expressions such as "hang ten" or "surf goofy foot." To "hang ten" means to grip the surfboard with all ten toes, and hang on. If you "surf goofy foot," it means that you surf with your left foot in front. (Usually surfers place their right foot ahead of the left when they stand on their boards.)

If you like fruit, you'll love this *ono* (delicious) Hawaiian dessert. It looks as good as it tastes! Remember to ask an adult for help.

HAWAIIAN TROPICAL DELIGHT

1/4 cup powdered sugar
36 miniature marshmallows
1/2 coconut, shredded and unsweetened
1 cup pineapple cubes, drained (fresh or canned)
1/2 chopped peeled mango (or drained canned peaches)
1/2 cup canned mandarin oranges, drained
2 teaspoons lemon juice
1 cup Cool Whip
1/4 cup extra coconut, sliced kiwi fruit, maraschino cherries (optional, for decoration)

1. Chill cream, then whip until stiff using an electric beater or hand whisk.
2. Using a metal spoon, gently stir pineapples, mango (or peaches), mandarin oranges, and coconut into cream.
3. Add sugar, marshmallows, and lemon juice.
4. Scoop Hawaiian Tropical Delight into glass dessert dishes, or empty coconut shells cut in half.
5. Sprinkle with extra shredded coconut and top with cherries. Decorate with kiwi slices.
6. Chill in refrigerator before serving. Serves 6–8.

popular ones among experienced surfers are the Banzai Pipeline, on O'ahu's North Shore, and Sandy Beach, on the southeast shore. Both beaches are dangerous, however, with strong currents and giant swells.

Serious surfers travel far and wide to find the perfect wave.

WORKING IN HAWAI'I

Hawai'i's main industry is tourism. More than 1 in 3 Hawaiian residents work in service industries that support the tourist trade. These jobs include hotel maids, kitchen and restaurant workers, skycaps, airline stewards, bank tellers, salesclerks, and taxi drivers.

Hawai'i's location in the middle of the Pacific Ocean makes it an important strategic site for American planes and ships to refuel or make repairs on their way west. For this reason, the federal government is one of the state's biggest employers. About 19,000 people work at Pearl Harbor Naval Shipyard, Hickam Air Force Base, Fort Shafter, Barbers Point, and other places. In fact, more people work for the federal government than any other employer.

One hundred years ago, agriculture was the state's biggest employer. The Big Five companies employed most of the labor force on their sugar and pineapple fields, or in their offices, packing plants, pineapple canneries, and mills. However, more recently, cheap imported sugar and pineapple from Taiwan and other places have forced many Hawaiian

The Dole Pineapple Cannery operated in Hawai'i until 1993.

pineapple and sugar plantations to close. Despite this, processed sugar and canned pineapple are still Hawai'i's chief manufactured goods. The manufacture of clothing, food, and printing are also important to the state's economy.

Island quarries employ several hundred workers in the production of crushed stone, cement, sand, and gravel. These nonfuel minerals are valued at $91.4 million. Commercial fishing accounts for another $65 million of the state's economy.

NATIVE HAWAIIANS TODAY

In the 1970s, Native Hawaiians experienced renewed interest in their culture, language, and politics. They began to express their pride in being Hawaiian or part Hawaiian. The Hawaiian language, crafts, and culture were revived.

Renewed Hawaiian pride led to an increased interest in learning the native Hawaiian language, which was in danger of becoming lost. Classes in Hawaiian were added to the University of Hawai'i curriculum. Hawaiian or part Hawaiian senior citizens, called kupuna, or elders, regularly visited classrooms to teach Hawaiian

EXTRA! EXTRA!

In 1973, the Polynesian Voyaging Society began building a double-hulled (two-bodied) Polynesian voyaging canoe using traditional Hawaiian methods. Two years later, manned by a crew of seventeen men, the canoe *Hokule'a* set sail from Kualoa, O'ahu. They sailed to the islands of Tahiti and back. The society wanted to prove that the first Polynesians to inhabit Hawai'i made the long journey between Tahiti and Hawai'i intentionally. They not only proved that it was possible, but they did so without using modern tools or navigational equipment.

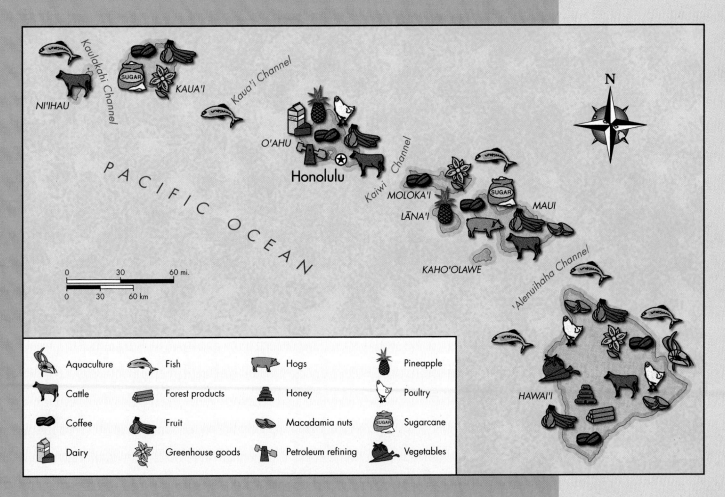

Honolulu

PACIFIC OCEAN

NI'IHAU

Kaulakahi Channel

KAUA'I

Kaua'i Channel

O'AHU

Kaiwi Channel

MOLOKA'I

LĀNA'I

MAUI

KAHO'OLAWE

'Alenuihaha Channel

HAWAI'I

N

0   30   60 mi.
0   30   60 km

	Aquaculture		Fish		Hogs		Pineapple
	Cattle		Forest products		Honey		Poultry
	Coffee		Fruit		Macadamia nuts		Sugarcane
	Dairy		Greenhouse goods		Petroleum refining		Vegetables

Island women use fresh palm leaves to make traditional Hawaiian decorative baskets.

crafts, Hawaiian mythology, and the Hawaiian language.

The beautiful weaving, hula dancing, music, and culture of old Hawai'i were also revived. Each year, *halaus,* or hula schools, compete in annual hula contests, such as the Merrie Monarch Festival in Hilo, or the Prince Lot hula festival on O'ahu. In May, there are lei-making contests to carry on the Hawaiian tradition of making flower or feather garlands. Competitions like these help to keep the Hawaiian culture alive and strong.

Anger and resentment toward the United States government have accompanied this renewed pride. Some Hawaiians have formed Hawaiian Sovereignty groups. The goal of these groups is to restore, or bring back, Hawaiian sovereignty, or rule by kings. They also believe that the overthrow of the Kingdom of Hawai'i was illegal, because the wishes of the Native Hawaiian people were not taken into consideration before the annexation. They feel that the United States government should repay Native Hawaiians for the islands that were annexed in 1893, in much the same way that Native American tribes have been repaid for their stolen lands.

In 1993, on the 100-year anniversary of the overthrow of the Hawaiian Kingdom, President Bill Clinton signed the Apology Bill. In this bill, the president officially apologized to Native Hawaiians for the United States government's actions during the overthrow.

Ni'ihau

We will start our tour of Hawai'i by visiting Ni'ihau. Before we climb aboard our helicopter for the short flight, we'll need an invitation from one of the islanders. No one can visit Ni'ihau without an invitation. That's why its nickname is the Forbidden Island.

The island of Ni'ihau was sold to the Sinclair family by King Kamehameha V in 1864 for $10,000 in gold. Ni'ihau has been privately owned by the Sinclairs' descendants, the Robinson family, ever since. Today, about 250 full-blooded Hawaiians live on the 70 square miles (181 sq km) of the island. They do not pay for their homes or their meat, which comes from the ranch. There are no phones or electricity on the island. Hawaiian is spoken at home and at school, where classes are taught only in Hawaiian from kindergarten to high school.

Ni'ihauans make their living from cattle and sheep ranching. They also string necklaces of rare *pupu,* delicate Ni'ihau shells, which are sold in gift shops. The island's rain forest contains many endangered plant species, which are fiercely protected by the island's owners.

Visitors can get an aerial view of Ni'ihau by taking a 3-hour helicopter tour.

53

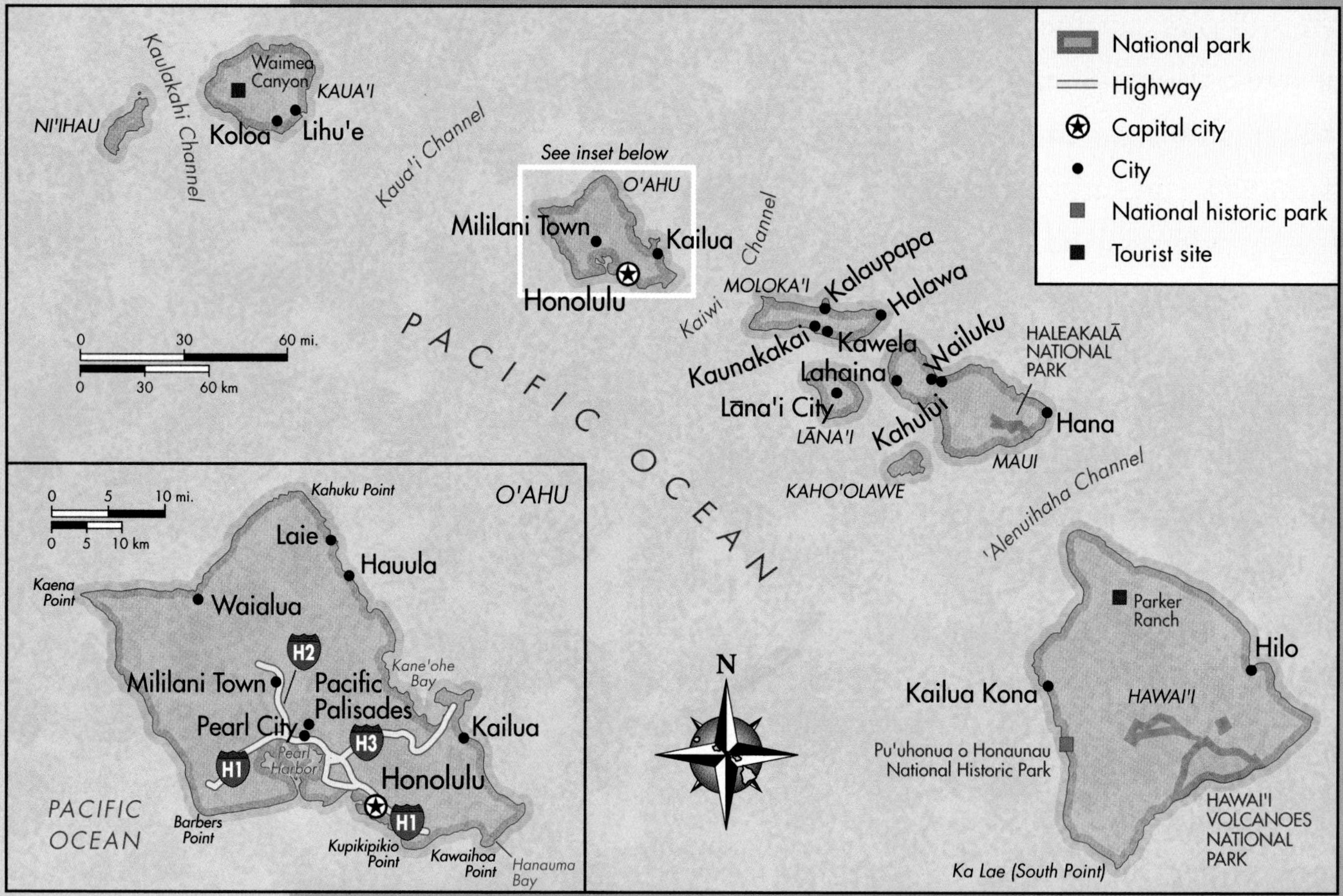

Map legend

- National park
- Highway
- ⊛ Capital city
- ● City
- ■ National historic park
- ■ Tourist site

Main map

NI'IHAU

Kaulakahi Channel

Waimea Canyon
KAUA'I
Koloa
Lihu'e

Kaua'i Channel

See inset below

O'AHU
Mililani Town
Kailua
Honolulu

Kaiwi Channel

Kailua Channel

MOLOKA'I
Kalaupapa
Halawa
Kaunakakai
Kawela
Wailuku
Lahaina
Lāna'i City
LĀNA'I
Kahului
MAUI
Hana

HALEAKALĀ NATIONAL PARK

KAHO'OLAWE

PACIFIC OCEAN

0   30   60 mi.
0   30   60 km

'Alenuihaha Channel

N

Parker Ranch
Kailua Kona
HAWAI'I
Hilo

Pu'uhonua o Honaunau National Historic Park

Ka Lae (South Point)

HAWAI'I VOLCANOES NATIONAL PARK

Inset map — O'AHU

O'AHU

0   5   10 mi.
0   5   10 km

Kahuku Point
Laie
Hauula
Kaena Point
Waialua
H2
Mililani Town
Pacific Palisades
Kane'ohe Bay
Pearl City
H3
Kailua
H1
Pearl Harbor
Honolulu
H1
PACIFIC OCEAN
Barbers Point
Kupikipikio Point
Kawaihoa Point
Hanauma Bay

Kaua'i

Kaua'i is Hawai'i's fourth largest island, with a land area of 550 square miles (1,424 sq km). Kaua'i is also called the Garden Island because of its breathtaking scenery. Thousands of coconut trees wave feather-duster fronds along the island's north shore. Steep cliffs called Na Pali rise like church steeples along the northwest coast. In fact, Kaua'i's amazing scenery was filmed for several movies. The jungles of *Jurassic Park,* the beaches of *Blue Hawai'i,* and scenes from *Raiders of the Lost Ark* are just a few of them.

Start your tour of the island by traveling a rough road up to Waimea Canyon. Sometimes called the Little Grand Canyon of the Pacific, Waimea Canyon is huge. It is 3,600 feet (1,097 m) deep and 2 miles (3.2 km) wide. This fault, or crack in the Earth's crust, cuts through 10 miles (16 km) of the Koke'e Mountains.

Rainbow colors seem to dance along the peaks of Waimea Canyon. The lines that appear on the canyon walls depict volcanic eruptions and lava flows over the centuries.

Next, head east to Wailua. On the way, you can catch glimpses of Kaua'i's most powerful rivers: the Wailuku River and the Hanalei River, a National Treasure. The valleys are lush and green. Not surprisingly, the wettest place in the world is directly above you, close to the source of these rivers. It is Mount Wai'ale'ale, 5,208 feet (1,587 m) above sea level. Its peaks receive more than 460 inches (1,168 cm) of rain each year.

Nearby is the Alakai Swamp, a National Wilderness Preserve. The swamp's tangled vegetation, deep bogs (marshes or swamps), and cool mists are home to more endangered Hawaiian bird and plant species than any other island. Environmentalists are working hard to preserve the Alakai Swamp so that its rare plant and bird species do not become extinct.

The small town of Wailua was Kaua'i's capital until it was moved to the old fashioned town of Lihue, farther south. After a quick visit to Koloa, to visit the state's first sugar mill, head south to Spouting Horn, not far from the end of the paved road. Getting soaked by the Horn's huge waterspout is a good way to cool off.

O'ahu

O'ahu is just across the Kaua'i Channel, east of Kaua'i. O'ahu is the third island in the chain. Although the meaning of its name is unknown, O'ahu is often called the Gathering Place. It was probably given this nickname because it is the most heavily populated island. More than 7 in every 10 people live on this island.

FIND OUT MORE

The northwestern islands are the habitat of the Hawaiian monk seal. Each year, the female monk seal comes to Kaua'i's beaches to give birth to her pups. Less than two hundred Hawaiian monk seal pups are born each breeding season. Sadly, many are eaten by sharks. Find out what is being done to save the Hawaiian monk seal from extinction.

Make your first stop in Pearl City, about 15 miles (24 km) north of Honolulu. Pearl City is home to Pearl Harbor, site of the Japanese attack in 1941. Take a short boat ride to the shining white *Arizona* Memorial. Most of the ship's 1,177 brave crewmen are still there, buried in their sunken ship.

Leaving Pearl Harbor, drive through the pineapple plantation town of Wahiawa. The rolling highway leads downhill between pineapple and coffee fields. Tall fields of waving green sugarcane grew there before there were coffee bushes. However, the Waialua Sugar Plantation and its mill have closed down.

Ahead are the sandy beaches of Haleiwa, Waimea Bay, Sunset, Ehukai, and other world-famous North Shore beaches. The Triple Crown of Surfing competition is held there every year. Surfing champions from Australia, South Africa, and other parts of the world come to the North Shore to surf the legendary Banzai Pipeline. This tricky but popular surfing spot challenges even the best surfers.

Waimea Falls and Valley Park is our next stop. There you can watch divers plunge off steep cliffs into the natural pool many feet below. Then go kayaking down the Waimea

The 184-foot- (56-m-) long memorial of the USS *Arizona* was built over the mid-portion (the hull) of the sunken battleship.

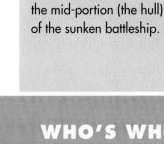

WHO'S WHO IN HAWAI'I?

Duke Paoa Kahanamoku (1890–1968) was an Olympic swimming champion and world-renowned surfer. Duke was known as the Father of International Surfing because he promoted the sport of surfing all over the world. His statue stands on Waikiki Beach. Kahanamoku was born in Honolulu.

A Hawaiian demonstrates the art of cracking a coconut at the Polynesian Cultural Center.

River, drive a dune buggy over a rugged course, or go horseback riding. The Waimea Valley, once home to an ancient Hawaiian village, is cool and shady and contains many unusual tropical plants. Parts of the village have been recreated for visitors to see.

The Polynesian Cultural Center is our next stop. There you can visit several South Pacific islands in the 40-acre (16-ha) park, including Hawai'i, Fiji, Samoa, the Marquesas, and New Zealand. Natives from each area demonstrate how to climb coconut trees, start fires without matches, weave mats, build huts, carve, or perform native dances. Try your hand at swinging Maori *poi-balls.* It's not as easy as it looks! Our long day at the Polynesian Cultural Center ends with a feast fit for a Hawaiian king or queen, and a lively Polynesian pageant in the center's theater.

After a night's rest, take Kahekili Highway to the Valley of the Temples. Deep in the valley is the lovely Byodo-In Temple, a serene red-roofed pagoda that is surrounded by towering mountains and fishponds. A smiling Buddhist priest in billowing robes lifts his arms to the sky. At once, dozens of tiny sparrows flutter down to perch on his shoulders, or to take food from his outstretched hands.

Sea Life Park is our next destination. The park is the home of the *wholphin,* Kekaimalu. This unusual animal is half dolphin and half whale. The park has an aquarium that contains hammerhead sharks, sea

At the Halona Blowhole, water sometimes shoots as far as 30 feet (9 m) into the air.

turtles, rays, brightly colored fish, and other sea creatures in a glass-walled natural habit. The dolphin training shows are fun to watch, too.

Back on the road again, drive past the Makapu'u Point lighthouse on your way to Halona Blowhole. Watch the water shoot up through a hole in the rocks, but stay safely behind the guardrail. The rocks and water are rough and very dangerous. Several people have drowned at the Blowhole because they ignored the warning signs.

Moloka'i

The beautiful island of Moloka'i is just across the Kaiwi Channel from O'ahu. Shaped like a shoe, Moloka'i is Hawai'i's fifth largest island. Moloka'i is home to Kahiwa Falls, one of the highest waterfalls in Hawai'i. The falls cascade 1,750 feet (533 m) over the world's steepest sea cliffs.

SPECIAL LANGUAGE

Hawaiian	English
hale	house
kai	salt water (ocean)
mahalo	thank you
maikai	good
makuakane	father
makua	mother
tutukane	grandfather
tutuwahine, tutu	grandmother

Moloka'i is a great place to go snorkeling or swimming, or to enjoy a sightseeing tour, complete with African wildlife. The friendly residents, beautiful scenery, and slow pace of life make the island of Moloka'i the perfect spot for a lazy vacation.

Lāna'i

Our next stop is Lāna'i, the most secluded (private) island in the chain. It is the sixth largest island, with an area of 140 square miles (363 sq km).

Hawaiian legend says that the boulders at Garden of the Gods were dropped from the sky by the gods tending their gardens.

Lāna'i City is the island's capital. Once a plantation town, Lāna'i City has a population of about 2,700. There are two hotels on the island, but no shopping malls. In fact, Lāna'i's only tourist attractions are its natural beauty, its crystal clear waters, and its peace and quiet. This makes Lāna'i very popular as a vacation spot for wealthy tourists from the city who want to get away from it all.

Follow a rocky dirt road to the Garden of the Gods. Lava rocks and boulders are scattered across the blood-red ground of this scenic spot. Although it looks as if someone carefully placed the boulders there, they are completely natural.

The island's highest point is Lāna'ihale. On a clear day, you can see many of the other islands from this windy ledge. Stop at Kahe'a and see the ruined heiau, an ancient Hawaiian temple, before heading back. The Luahiwa Petroglyphs are in the opposite direction. These are interesting stick figures of people and animals that were chipped from the rocks by early Hawaiians.

Wild deer, bighorn sheep, the Hawaiian hoary bat, and many types of birds are found on Lāna'i, including pheasants and wild turkeys. Hawaiian green sea turtles often visit Lāna'i. However, they always return to French Frigate Shoals, 1,000 miles (1,609 km) north of Hawai'i, to breed.

Kaho'olawe

Kaho'olawe is just 45 square miles (117 sq km) and is uninhabited. One hundred years ago, Kaho'olawe was used to graze sheep, cattle, and goats. Overgrazing by these animals destroyed the vegetation that grew on the island. The plants were never able to recover because Kaho'olawe is in Maui's "rainshadow," or directly behind Maui. The clouds drop all of their moisture on Maui, leaving none for Kaho'olawe.

Despite its lack of vegetation and fresh water, Native Hawaiians consider Kaho'olawe a place of great cultural, spiritual, and historical significance. Certain areas of the island were used by early Hawaiians in the making of weapons. Other areas are the sites of heiaus, or ancient shrines.

From 1941 to 1994, Kaho'olawe was used as a target for bombing practice by the U.S. Navy, despite protests by Native Hawaiians. Since the bombing ended in 1994, the Navy has worked to remove unexploded missiles from the island. The general public is still not allowed to visit Kaho'olawe because of possible dangers.

Native Hawaiians are currently working to re-establish Kaho'olawe's cultural and spiritual sites. Native Hawaiians hope that eventually they will be able to live on the island as their ancestors once did.

Maui

Our next stop is Maui, which has an area of 730 square miles (1,891 sq km). The island is actually two inactive volcanos connected by an isthmus, or strip of land. It is this valley that gave the island its nickname, the Valley Isle.

First visit Haleakalā, the dormant volcano to the east of the island. Haleakalā, which means "house of the sun," is a great place to watch the sun rise. If you feel cold and a little dizzy as you drive higher, it is because of the altitude (height above sea level). Haleakalā is just over 10,000 feet (3,048 m) above sea level. Sometimes the clouds are so low you can jump right through them.

Clouds rise up to meet the rim of Haleakalā Crater at 9,000 feet (2,743 m).

The entire crater of Haleakalā Volcano is a National Park. From the lookout point, you can see rocks in a rainbow of red, orange, black, and brown. These colors gave the crater its nickname, Pele's Paintbox. The park is also home to a rare plant called the silversword, and the endangered nene goose.

The handsome brown, black, and cream nene (*nay-nay*) is Hawai'i's official state bird. Unlike other geese, which have webbed feet for swimming, the nene's feet are only partially webbed because it lives on land. Its claws help the nene to get around its rocky habitat. The nene also has shorter wings than other geese.

After a long drive down the mountain, we come to Lahaina, on the island's north-west coast. Lahaina was once the capital of the Hawaiian Kingdom. When the first whaling ships came to the islands in 1819, Lahaina became a busy whaling port. So many whales were killed during this time that the humpback whale, Hawai'i's official marine animal, was nearly driven to extinction. Today, U.S. law protects the humpback whale.

Silverswords grow only at Haleakalā Crater. They flower just once before dying.

Female whales come to Maui each winter to give birth to their young. Whale babies, called calves, are 10 feet (3 m) long and weigh more than 2,500 pounds (1,134 kilograms) at birth. Visitors to Maui often take whale-watching tours to study humpback whales. The sight of a whale shooting water from its blowhole is unforgettable.

Hawai'i

The island of Hawai'i gave its name to the entire state. It lies to the east of Maui, across the 'Alenuihaha Channel. Hawai'i's nickname, the Big Island, is a good one—Hawai'i is twice as big as the other islands added together.

The Big Island was created by the eruptions of several volcanoes: Mauna Kea, Mauna Loa, Hualalai, Kohala, and Kilauea Iki. Kilauea is an active volcano that is part of Hawai'i Volcanoes National Park. In fact, Kilauea is the most active volcano in the world. Its lava flows have added almost 600 acres (243 ha) of new land to the island's coast since 1983. The Big Island is getting even bigger!

Although it is beautiful, an eruption can also be very dangerous. Lava flowing from Kilauea has destroyed more than two hundred homes and an ancient Hawaiian temple on the volcano's southeast slopes. Several beaches have also been buried under the lava flows.

Next, hike down the Chain of Craters Road. The road circles the volcano's older, dormant craters, or caldera. (A crater is the hole through which lava explodes during an eruption.) There are steam vents where wisps of steam escape through natural cracks in the ground from the volcano below. Sulfur from the eruption makes the steam smell like rotten eggs.

At Hawai'i Volcanoes National Park, lava fields of black volcanic rubble stretch for miles in every direction.

Another good place to explore is the Thurston lava tube. A lava tube is a long cave, like a tunnel. Lava tubes are created when the outside edges of a lava flow become cool and harden, but the middle section stays liquid and keeps moving. This creates a hollow tube, or cave, in the lava. Ancient Hawaiians used lava tubes as burial caves for the bones of their chieftains, so be quiet and respectful as you pass through them.

Travel west to Mauna Loa, the Long Mountain. Mauna Loa is the state's second highest volcano at 13,679 feet (4,169 m). Another 18,000 feet (5,486 m) of the mountain are hidden beneath the ocean. If measured from below sea level, Mauna Loa is the biggest mountain in the world, at 33,476 feet (10,204 meters).

Mauna Loa is one of Earth's most active volcanoes. It has erupted 33 times since 1843.

Northeast of Mauna Loa is Mauna Kea, the White Mountain. At 13,796 feet (4,205 m) above sea level, it is the Big Island's highest mountain. Astronomers, or scientists who study the stars, come from eleven different countries to do research at the observatories there. The elevation and the clear, clean air make it one of the best places in the world to study the stars.

One of the observatories is the W. M. Keck Observatory. Since 1992, the Keck Observatory has used the world's most powerful telescopes. One of these, the Keck I telescope, is over 80 feet (24 m) tall and weighs 300 tons (272 metric tons). Its mirror is 33 feet (10 m) in diameter.

The Keck telescopes track stellar objects for hours at a time.

Next, head into the rolling green hills of the Kohala Mountains. Tiny white churches with pointed spires are tucked into the hills. Blue morning glory vines spill over old lava-rock walls. Each afternoon, a cool misty rain fills the air. Nearby, close to Kamuela, is the Parker Ranch. The ranch was once the world's largest cattle ranch owned by one person, John Parker, and his descendants. More than 55,000 cattle graze the ranch's hilly pastures. They are still herded by paniolo on horseback.

From the Parker Ranch, drive east to the Hamakua Coast. Unlike Kona, the eastern side of the Big Island is lush and green, with rainforests and waterfalls. Sugarcane was once the biggest industry there, but in the last ten years many sugar plantations have gone out of business. There are several macadamia nut, anthurium, and orchid flower farms in the area, however. In fact, the Big Island produces more macadamia nuts and orchids than any other place in the world.

Next, drive southeast to the town of Hilo. It rains in Hilo almost every day. In fact, with 130 inches (330 cm) of rain per year, Hilo is the wettest town in the United States. A good time to visit Hilo is during the weekly open-air fruit and vegetable market. The market is a sea of beautiful colors. You'll find tubs of red anthuriums; red, yellow and pink torch ginger; yellow, white, and purple orchids; golden papayas; red mangoes; and yellow bananas.

EXTRA! EXTRA!

In the past, Hilo has endured the terrible effects of tsunamis. *Tsunami* is a Japanese word meaning "harbor wave." Earthquakes or volcanic eruptions create giant waves. Tsunamis can travel across the ocean at speeds of up to 500 miles per hour (805 kph). When they touch land, these giant waves destroy everything in their path. In April 1946, a 56-foot (17-m) tidal wave crashed over Hilo, killing 159 people. In 1960, another tsunami claimed 61 lives.

Downtown Hilo features unique shops and restaurants.

Below Hilo, in the southern central part of the Big Island, is the district of Kau, an area of forests and deserts. Kau's southernmost tip is called South Point, or Ka Lae. South Point is farther south than any other place in the United States.

Our final stop is Pu'uhonua o Honaunau, a National Historic Park. In ancient times, a *pu'uhonua* was a refuge, or safe place, for Native Hawaiians who broke a law. These people could be killed unless they reached the pu'uhonua without getting caught. Today, the refuge is still there, guarded by fierce-looking *tikis*. These carved wooden statues represent the ancient Hawaiian gods of nature and creation.

We've come to the end of our island tour. Hawai'i is a beautiful and interesting state. It is an island paradise full of adventure and breathtaking scenery. *Aloha!*

HAWAI'I ALMANAC

Statehood date and number: August 21, 1959/50th

State seal: The state seal is patterned after the royal coat of arms of the Hawaiian Kingdom. It features King Kamehameha the Great on one side and the Goddess of Liberty on the other, holding the Hawaiian flag. A sun rises in the background and the year 1959 is printed on top, indicating the year of statehood. A star is in the center of the shield, and a phoenix is below the shield. The state motto is written around the bottom of the seal. Originally designed in 1895.

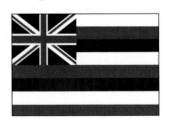

State flag: Great Britain's red, white, and blue Union Jack in the top-left corner against a red, white, and blue striped background. The eight stripes represent the eight major Hawaiian islands. Adopted in 1816.

Geographic center: Off Maui island, 20° 15' N, 156° 20' W

Total area/rank: 6,470 square miles (16,757 sq km)/47th

Coastline/rank: 750 miles (1,206 km)/4th

Latitude and longitude: Hawai'i is located approximately between 18° 55' and 28° 25' N and 154° 48' and 178° 25' W.

Highest/lowest elevation: 13,796 feet (4,205 m) at Mauna Kea/sea level at the Pacific Ocean

Hottest/coldest temperature: 100° F (38° C) at Pahala on April 27, 1931/12° F (–11° C) on Mauna Kea on May 17, 1979

Land area/rank: 6,423 square miles (16,636 sq km)/47th

Inland water area: 45 square miles (117 sq km)

Population/rank (2000 census): 1,211,537/42nd

Population of major city:

Honolulu: 371,657

Origin of state name: The Polynesians called it *Hawaiki*, after the homeland they had left behind.

State capital: Honolulu

Counties: 4

State government: 25 senators, 51 representatives

Major rivers: Wailuku, Hanalei, Wailua

Farm products: Sugar-cane, pineapples, flowers

Livestock: Cattle, hogs, poultry

Manufactured products: Processed sugar, canned pineapple, clothing, food, printing

Mining products: Crushed stone, cement, sand, gravel

Fishing products: Tuna, swordfish, mahi mahi

Bird: Nene goose

Fairs/festivals: Aloha Week Parade, Kamehameha Day Parade

Fish: Humuhumunukunuku apua'a, the trigger fish

Flower: Yellow hibiscus

Fruit: Pineapple

Grass: *Pili,* or bunch grass

Marine mammal: Humpback whale

Motto: *"Ua mau ke ea o ka aina I ka pono"* or "The life of the land is perpetuated in righteousness."

Nickname: The Aloha State

Tree: *Kukui,* or candlenut tree

Song: "Hawai'i Pono'i," written by King David Kalākaua

TIMELINE

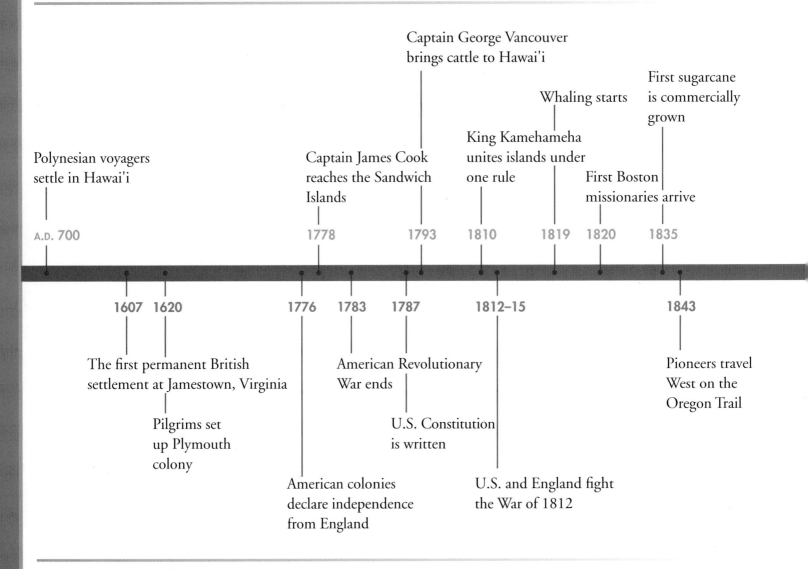

HAWAI'I STATE HISTORY

Captain George Vancouver
brings cattle to Hawai'i

First sugarcane
is commercially
grown

Whaling starts

King Kamehameha
unites islands under
one rule

Polynesian voyagers
settle in Hawai'i

Captain James Cook
reaches the Sandwich
Islands

First Boston
missionaries arrive

A.D. 700   1778   1793   1810   1819 1820   1835

1607 1620   1776   1783   1787   1812–15   1843

The first permanent British
settlement at Jamestown, Virginia

American Revolutionary
War ends

Pioneers travel
West on the
Oregon Trail

Pilgrims set
up Plymouth
colony

U.S. Constitution
is written

American colonies
declare independence
from England

U.S. and England fight
the War of 1812

UNITED STATES HISTORY

Above the timeline:

Queen Lili'uokalani
is overthrown

King Liholiho
proclaims new
law called the
Great Mahele

Hawaiian Kingdom
becomes a U.S.
territory

Hawai'i becomes the
fiftieth state

Hurricane Iniki hits
Kaua'i

Hawaiian astronaut Onizuka
is killed in *Challenger* disaster

President Bill
Clinton signs the
Apology Bill

Japan bombs Pearl Harbor

Timeline (top dates): 1848 · 1893 · 1900 · 1941 · 1959 · 1986 · 1992 · 1993

Timeline (bottom dates): 1846–48 · 1861–65 · 1917–18 · 1929 · 1941–45 · 1950–53 · 1964 · 1965–73 · 1969 · 1991 · 1995

Below the timeline:

U.S. fights
war with
Mexico

Civil War
occurs in the
United States

U.S. takes part in
World War I

The stock market
crashes and U.S.
enters the Great
Depression

U.S. fights in
World War II

U.S. fights in the
Korean War

Civil rights laws
passed in the U.S.

U.S. fights in the
Vietnam War

Neil Armstrong
and Edwin
Aldrin land on
the moon

U.S. and other nations
fight in Persian Gulf War

U.S. space
shuttle
docks with
Russian
space station

GALLERY OF FAMOUS HAWAIIANS

Tia Carrere
(1967–)
Former model turned actress. Her movies include *Wayne's World* and *True Lies.* Born in Honolulu.

Sanford Ballard Dole
(1844–1926)
President of Hawaiian republic and first territorial governor. He was leader of the annexationists and led the takeover of Hawai'i in 1893. Born at Punahou.

Don Ho
(1930–)
World renowned Hawaiian entertainer. He is best known for the song "Tiny Bubbles." Born in Honolulu.

Jason Scott Lee
(1966–)
Famous actor of Chinese-Hawaiian ancestry. Jason starred in several movies, including *The Jungle Book* and *Dragon: The Bruce Lee Story.* Lives in Pearl City.

Bette Midler
(1945–)
Well-known singer and actress. Her movies include *The First Wives Club, Beaches,* and *The Rose.* One of her most popular recordings is "Wind Beneath My Wings." Born in Honolulu.

Ellison Onizuka
(1946–1986)
First Hawaiian to become a NASA astronaut. Lieutenant-Colonel Onizuka was killed in 1986, when the *Challenger* space shuttle exploded shortly after liftoff. The Ellison Onizuka Space Center in Kona was built in his honor. Born in Kealakekua.

Keali'i Reichel
(1962–)
Popular Hawaiian singer. Won seventeen Na Hoku Hanohano Awards from the Hawaiian music industry. His recordings often reach national charts, and his concerts are popular worldwide. Born on Maui.

GLOSSARY

ahupua'a: the portion of land allocated to each extended family, which reached from the mountain to the sea

aloha: hello, goodbye, love

dormant: sleeping, not active

harpoon: to stab with a spear thrown or fired from a boat

heiau: sacred Hawaiian ground temple for agriculture or sacrifice

hula: graceful dance of hand motions and swaying hips

leprosy: a disfiguring disease causing lumps on the skin

missionary: person who travels abroad to spread religious faith

molten: melted into a liquid

monarchy: a state ruled by kings and queens

navigate: to direct the course of a ship or aircraft

plantation: a large farm on which a crop such as sugar-cane, cotton, tea, etc. is grown

pu'uhonua: place of refuge (Hawaiian)

shoal: part of a river, sea, lake, etc. where the water is very shallow

translate: to change from one form of speech or written language to another

tsunami: tidal wave (Japanese)

FOR MORE INFORMATION

Web sites

Hawai'i Visitors and Convention Bureau
http://www.gohawaii.com
The official tourism web site of Hawai'i.

eHawaiiGov
http://www.state.hi.us/
The official web site of the Hawaiian government.

Hawai'i Volcanoes National Park
http://www.nps.gov/havo/home.htm
Information about the history of the park and its ecosystems.

Books

Juvik, James O., Sonia P. Juvik, and Thomas R. Paradise. *Student Atlas of Hawai'i.* Honolulu, HI: The Bess Press, 2000.

Linnea, Sharon. *Princess Ka'iulani: Hope of a Nation, Heart of a People.* Grand Rapids, MI: William B. Eerdmans Publishing, 1999.

McGowen, Tom. *The Attack on Pearl Harbor.* Danbury, CT: Children's Press, 2002.

Nicolson, Cynthia Pratt. *Volcano!* Kids Can Press, 2001.

Addresses

Governor of Hawai'i
Executive Chambers
Hawai'i State Capitol
Honolulu, HI 96813

Hawai'i Visitors and Convention Bureau
2270 Kalakaua Avenue, 8th Floor
Honolulu, HI 96815

INDEX

ABOUT THE AUTHOR

P. J. Neri is the creator of *Hawai'i Chillers* and the *Diamond Head High Series,* two best-selling fiction series for island children and teens. She has also written more than twenty-seven historical novels for adults. Born in Suffolk, England, Neri lives in Mililani, Hawai'i, with her husband and their two dogs, Heidi and Holly. Before writing this book, she read everything she could find about her home state of Hawai'i. She loves living in the Aloha State. Neri says, "Hawai'i no ka oi!" or "Hawai'i is the best!" *Aloha!*

Photographs © 2003: Amelia Hill: 66 top; AP/Wide World Photos/Ronen Zilberman: 74 bottom left; Archive Photos/Getty Images: 35; Brown Brothers: 31; Corbis Images: 50, 53 (James L. Amos), 20, 33 top (Bettmann), 49 (Rick Doyle), 74 top right, 74 top left (Mitchell Gerber), 17 (Historical Picture Archive), 60 (David Muench), 46 (Douglas Peebles), 67 (Roger Ressmeyer), 59 (David Samuel Robbins), 63 (Kevin Schafer), 58 (Phil Schermeister), 12 (Jay Syverson), 29 (UPI), 74 bottom right (Michael S. Yamashita), 24 top, 33 bottom; Dave G. Houser/HouserStock, Inc.: 21; David R. Frazier: 13, 37, 39, 70 top left, 71 bottom right; Dembinsky Photo Assoc.: 57 top, 70 right (Howard L. Garrett), 71 top left (Darrell Gulin), 65 (Adam Jones); Douglas Peeples Photography: 56, 64 (Michael S. Nolan), 44, 45; Getty Images: 36 (Evan Agostini), 71 top right (Frank Wing); Hulton|Archive/Getty Images: 57 bottom; MapQuest.com, Inc.: 70 bottom left; Network Aspen/John Russell: 14, 22; North Wind Picture Archives: 16, 19, 23, 24 bottom, 25, 26, 30; Photo Researchers, NY/Stephen J. Krasemann: 71 bottom left; Robert Fried Photography: 42, 47, 52; Steve Mulligan Photography: 3 right, 55; Stone/Getty Images: 68 (Bruce Forster), 8 (G. Brad Lewis); Terry Donnelly: 7, 11, 62; The Image Works/James Marshall: 3 left, 4; Tom Till Photography, Inc.: cover; Unicorn Stock Photos/Jeff Greenberg: 38; Visuals Unlimited/Bruce S. Cushing: 66 bottom.